The Dual Career
Real Estate Agent

To Be Or Not To Be?

By

Wanda Russell

The Dual Career Real Estate Agent

To Be Or Not To Be?

Copyright © 2017 Wanda Russell

ISBN-13: 978-1973964339

ISBN-10: 1973964333

Published by *Buckner Enterprises Unlimited* ® 2016
Waldorf, Maryland 301.458.5767

Contents

Introduction

I have been a dual career real estate agent for more than twenty years, (working a full-time nine to five job, as we call it) creating and maintaining the volume and income as if I was only doing real-estate as a full-time agent (no 9 to 5 job). I would often just stop and think "what is the definition of fulltime in the real estate world?" I see all real estate agents as full-time if you are working your real estate business more than thirty hours a week. I will share with you what my day looks like and techniques I use to accomplish the volume of an agent that only works real estate fulltime not as a dual career agent. Over the years I have developed, tested and currently use the following techniques. But first you have to determine if you are full-time or not. You do not have to have core hours, just any time spent in your business over thirty or more hours a week in my opinion could be considered full-time.

For the reading purposes:
- Full-time: Only doing real estate
- Dual Career: Working a 9 to 5 and doing real estate after work and weekends.

If you are to increase your income and business of any type you must put the time in and be passionate about what you are doing. When you are passionate about what you are doing, time will get away from you and it will never feel like a job. I will often say to myself that I am training for the business Olympics. I look at how the athletes train for the Olympics, putting in over twelve hours or more a day to perfect their craft. When you want something bad enough you will make the sacrifices to be the best that you can be whether building a business or becoming number one in the passion that you have inside of you.

I have been fortunate enough to receive a few awards within my brokerage and affiliated professional board based on my production. Having received awards based on production gave me visibility among my peers and colleagues within real estate profession that are working a nine to five and then real estate in the afternoon and weekends. Having been given that visibility opened me up to the question of "How am I doing the production along with my full-time, nine to five job?"

Almost daily as I walk through my real estate office, one of my colleagues or a student of the real estate school stops me and asks how I am doing it. How do I keep a full-time job and make the income and build the client base as if I only do real estate full-time. There are also times when they find out that I am not completely full-time and they want to do lunch to find out how I rank among my peers in volume as if I am a full-time agent (not dual career agent). If I took the time to go out for lunch, or just stop to talk in the office about my techniques I would never be able to keep up with my standard of production.

I started to think about the time I spent explaining concepts, procedures, and techniques that I use to all that stop me and it was becoming time lost for my production and overwhelming. It dawned on me one day that there is a need for a written guide to share my techniques that can help individual agents and brokerage centers grow. I started interviewing brokerage centers and individual agents to help me to determine the percentage of dual career agents and what I found are there are sometimes more dual career agents coming in after their nine to five jobs than agents that are there in the office all day. The ratio of full-time agents to dual career agents being higher may not be completely true for all just the ones that I have visited and asked the question. If the brokerage centers that have the highest percentage of dual career agents can get them polished up with the techniques, skills, and procedures to change their mind set and or implement procedures that could increase their productivity and could possibly see a game changer on how dual career agent are viewed in the business world no matter the business type. This could only create a win-win for the brokerage and the agents personally.

When I decided to write this guide of techniques I became hesitant because I am not a writer and it would take time away from my time that I would be serving my clients and customers. Now that I am putting it on paper I determined that it may help me to fine tune and come up with more techniques to test and also if it could help an agent or business owner follow their dreams it will be all worth it.

I wanted to make this a quick and easy read. It is not my intention to put a lot of fluff in this writing just my story of techniques, processes and procedures that I use to maintain the level of business that has peeked the curiosity of other real estate agents. I hope this guide will help you to increase your business and production because that is my intent.

Secret Agent

I had to learn to be a secret agent and dual career agent because of my job and how clients will view their service with me. If my clients knew I worked a full-time job as a dual career agent, they will already program their minds that they would not receive top notch customers service or I will not be available to show them houses when they are available. I learned how to get around that mind set of clients and customers by never letting them know that I have a full-time job so I became a secret agent. I remember saying to myself that if they are buying a home they are probably at work during the same core working hours that I have so having a full-time job never affected my business.

I also learned that you can never change the mind set of your clients or customers so I had to keep to myself any family emergency or any activity that will change their idea of what to expect of me as a realtor. I remember when my father passed away I had at least three deals preparing to go to settlement and did not have realtor support and did not want my clients to think I would drop the ball on their deal so, I continue to work through it with the use of technology. I remember being in South Carolina without them knowing it and emailing, and making phone call to keep all the deals going from the funeral home still conducting business with my family and my clients. I learned early on that my emergency if I could help it should not bring fear of service to others. I do know there may be a time that I may have to let others know of emergency but at that time I did what I had to do to provide excellent customer service and not bring fear to my clients in one of the biggest transaction of their lives. I now have support which will allow me to step back if I need to.

With my full-time job I had to be careful and selective as to who knew what I did after work and on weekends. I had to be a top-secret agent in the earlier years of my career. I know how people can see you when they think you don't need money because of what the possibilities could be if my business grew. Knowing that I was building a business, the money was not as I wanted it to be but I could not change the perception that others, coworkers or supervisors would have about me and how successful I was or could be. The promotion for performance on my job may never come if they had a jealous bone in their body because they may think I don't need it even though I deserved it. I always put on my resume that I have a real estate license but I don't think they remember reading it.

I could not control if someone found out I was a real estate agent, but I never put it in their face, they would have had to just find out. I am very selective of whom I did reveal myself to and with that I ask a higher power to show me and whisper to me who the individuals would be. I never really used social media or did a lot of advertising that was visible. My business grew based on customer service and customer service referrals. I will let my clients know that they could call me at any time seven days a week and Sunday after church. Today I still live by my customer service rule of the seven days a week and Sunday after church. If I were going to build my business I had to make some sacrifices and the sacrifices was time. If I was at work Monday through Friday the only time I could build my business was after work and the weekends.

The closer I get to retirement I have started doing just a little social media for clients and potential clients to see where my passion lies but still not letting them know that I have a full-time job. I will stay a secret agent until I walk away from my full-time job. You can be very successful as a dual career- agent, you just have to pick your battles. I still to this day chose to be a secret, dual career agent so I do not have to fight battles while building my business.

I am not a secret agent when I am away from work. The ability to talk with people on the street became my way of generating leads. I will shout it from the roof tops metaphorically at my son school, food store, church, family gathering etc. I think you get the picture.

I learned early on with building my real estate business you have to learn when to hold them or when to fold them and allow yourself the ability to accept the effects it could have on your success, remembering all things have its season of harvest. Even being a secret, dual career agent I was just as successful as a full-time agent.

Dual Purpose Actions

Pushing me to discover the dual purpose action process comes from having others trying to convince me to become a full-time agent and give up my full-time nine to five job. The questions they challenged me with from time to time pushed me only harder to discover a way to have the best of both worlds because that is what I wanted for now. The statement from full-time agents that also would come up would be "If you did this full-time you could probably triple your income because you will be focusing all your energy to being that agent".

Why are there so many dual career agents? Now that is the question (to be or not to be). I know for me I am close to retirement and receiving full benefits for the rest of my life more important to me right now. As I talk with colleagues for some it was a list of responses as to why they choose to work both as a real-estate sales agent and maintain their 9 to 5 as we call it. Some of the reasons that I heard was the fear of not having the consistent income that would come in no matter what the economy is doing, having the security of having benefits for themselves and their families with no worries, not being disciplined to put away for retirement and not having the family support based of their fears and the unknowns of the universe.

From time to time I have seen agents go through tough times when it comes to their income based on expenses that come up with their family, business expenses, and or just life events and it creates stress and anxiety. Talking with my colleagues as they may express to me their financial storms I would say to them why not get a job or maybe just a part time job and they will reply no that is not an option. It would always challenge my belief as to why they would not get a job if only just temporarily. I also have colleagues that say it is all or nothing and they do extremely well and blow all expectations to all or nothing to a whole other level and are doing extremely well. So, for me this is my opinion, everyone has their own destiny and we have to own it no matter what.

I have continuously created ways to master all the actions in my business as dual purpose which allows me to maximize my time, to still have some time for myself and my family. There is one thing you want to be conscience of is that you should always have time for yourself and your family because without them wealth or income with no one to share it with can be no fun. I have tried to master the techniques that I use to allow me to receive a high rate of return in more than one way per actions. Time management is designed to increase your business and your income for doing business. I don't focus on the income I just focus on my techniques. The challenge is the actions that I have to perform to keep up with the full-time agent schedule and their ability to do what I can't do because I am at work has allowed me to look deep into what can I do to produce the same end result as the full-time agent. I will share just a few of them with you so you can have an idea of what I have done over the years.

I start early in the day which allows me to get tasks completed before going to my nine to five. I start my day job at 6am and work a 9-hour day which allows me to have one day off each pay period every two weeks. I typically get into my real-estate office around 3:30 to 4pm each day. Think about it, if someone is a client they are possibly working close to the same core hours that I work. If clients are at work also so they will not typically miss you or your service. I normally take my lunch time to make or return calls from clients, I only have 30 min for lunch so there is no time to be with other coworkers for lunch, the dual purpose action is eating lunch and returning and making phone calls. Most jobs give you 2 breaks of 15 minutes each which could also allow you the opportunity to make calls or go over your tasks for when you get off work while walking to get exercise and clear your head.

If you have doctor's appointments, make them on the day you have a settlement schedule so you don't have to take off from work more than once. As your business grows, you will find that you can take off for each transaction so in order to maintain your leave balance on job, schedule the settlements later in the day or on the days of your doctor's appointments.

If you work a flexible schedule on your job then make sure on your regular scheduled day off you maximize it with activates for yourself and your business. I take my day off to workout at the gym and network while there, attending real estate events, lead generating and just catching up on paperwork and business development.

I normally door knock when I am waiting on a client to show. If you have a client that you have scheduled a showing for and asked you to meet them at the property go early or if you have to wait on them because they are running late then always have flyers to pass out in the area (waiting on client and marketing and exercising at the same time). I find the ability to market with flyers or door knocking also allows me the opportunity to exercise while completing the marketing or lead generation task.

Sometimes I may take my lunch time at my nine to five to make cold calls to past clients and future perspective clients (lunch and cold calling) As you can see there could be many ways to create dual action items that will allow you to grow your business and have some of the same results as a full-time agent.

Adjust

There are many times I would prepare a to do list for the day or as we call it a schedule and within 3 hours of the day I need to change it. I have learned to just adjust because my client's needs come first. If you learn to adjust then you will not be stress out. I learn to just roll with it and as my brother would all ways say it will work itself out. I never understood what that meant when my brother said it but now I do and I find myself more relaxed in each situation.

I start my days early even on the weekends because after about 10am the clients are up and on the move and you as the agent will become a part of their schedule. I try to get as much done on Saturday mornings before 9am with the expectation of making adjustments when the phone starts to ring remembering now my clients are maximizing their time during the weekend so tag I am it.

As a dual career agent I have been able to serve as many as 4 clients on one given day and that day is normally a Saturday. I may start my day as early as 6am which allows me the opportunity to organize showing and meeting with clients based on service required or urgency. I have learned to schedule showings in location blocks which allow me to maximize time and the ability to show multiple homes. If the client cancels the appointment I will already have prepared other clients I can call to service or office and paper work I can do so I can again maximize time with the adjustment.

If you look up the word adjust, it is a verb and means to alter or move (something) slightly in order to achieve the desired fit, appearance, or result. Learn how to accept the direction that you are pushed in and start tracking the results and you will see you may just become more comfortable with the ability to adjust.

Being a dual career agent, I had to learn over time to just adjust more and more as my business grew. I was so overwhelmed at one point in my real estate career that I got concerned that I might drop the ball on one of my clients or lose them as a client because I could only do one thing at a time or be one place at a time. I meet with my clients so we can build the relationship and introduce the teamwork expectation before providing service. Meeting with the potential client is time well spent. It allows me the time to understand the style of home and their communication style that best fits them. Meeting with the client allows me to make fewer adjustments because all expectations on both sides are up front. I am not saying there won't be adjustments but it should help keep the adjustments to a minimal.

If you run into a road block and it is facing you head on and you can't go through it, you may have to adjust and go around it. So often we complain, moan and groan about the obstacle but it could just be a stepping stone if you choose to use it that way. Learn to look at your adjustments as a GPS rerouting and you can get to the end result or your destination if you just make the adjustments and keep it moving.

Family Ties

I know it can be hard being a dual career agent and then adding family responsibilities with it. I am not saying that adding a third activity or responsibility will be easy, but I know it can be done. I did real estate when my son was in middle school and now he is a grown man and has now joined me in the real estate business. It was not easy but I did it. So, I am saying you can do it while you grow your business and family relationships.

Often my colleagues and family members will ask me where I find all my energy to do what I do back then and especially now because I am getting older. I believe that what you put your mind to do you could do it but it starts with believing in yourself, part DNA, passion and support. If you don't believe in yourself, others will feel your weakness and may not provide the support that you need. The DNA part come from your parents or ancestors, that possessed the talents in which you now possess. That's why some DNA traits you use in your business comes naturally. If we look at the passion part of it when you enjoy what you do it could just possibly come naturally because you just may be working in your destiny of what you were created to do. We all have talents and when you discover what they are just incorporate your family into your business and watch it grow just as a plant that needs water for nutrients you must feed yourself first and then your family. They will see and reap the benefits and with that comes support.

I learned early in my real estate career that when you involve your family they will have a better understanding of what you do or have to go through to get results or rate of return on the time spent away from home or family activities. When you are a dual career agent you will spend a lot of time away from home so when you can have them help you. I remember having my husband help me with driving around looking at homes as I preview for my clients and again back to being a dual action item (husband and I spending time together) still working the business. At my son's sports events, I use that time to network with other parents as well as being there for our son. The only thing different from me and the other parents would be that my conversation was business related and my son did not care about the conversation the only thing he cared about is that I was there. These are just a few examples of how I incorporated family time to grow my business while working as a dual career agent. When attending the sports events for my son I was not a secret agent. The sports events allowed me the opportunity to lead generate (market for new clients) and support my son (dual purposed action).

Time Management

One of the most important elements of being a dual career agent is time management. Time management skills can be natural or learned but the key will be that you know what is important to the achieving results. I often have colleagues come to me after finding out that I have a full-time job because I have mastered the illusion of being in the office as a full-time agent. The illusion of being in the office is no more than mastering time management. The ability to multi task, prioritize and adjust are the key elements that I use to master time management.

I work in an environment that allows me to have one day off every two weeks so I chose Wednesday as my day off when 95% of all workers take a Friday or a Monday as their day off. When it came time for me to choose my day over seventeen years ago I chose Wednesday. My colleagues laughed at me saying that there was something wrong with me. I had a plan to be successful in my full-time job as well as in my real estate business as a dual career agent. I learned early on that if most people working in this area are off on Mondays or Fridays, I could risk running into them and they could find out about my career in real estate. You can't completely hide or be a secret agent but I never wanted to flaunt it. I also found out that I can get more things done personal because most people were at work on those days and I could maximize my time to complete personal task like car repairs and home repairs.

My reasoning for picking the middle of the week would be that it would provide the illusion that I was in the office and it was not the typical day off for most. Also having the middle of the week off is more of a business day than a Monday or a Friday. On Monday people are surviving the remnants of the weekend and on Friday they are preparing for the weekend. I took the time to monitor when most settlements, home inspection and real estate task took place in my business and study showed for me that Wednesday show elevated levels for real estate task for my business. I think back to what my colleagues said about me for choosing a Wednesday and not Monday or Friday but I knew I chose the best day for me and it clearly is working because still most of my colleagues and clients don't know that I have a full-time job because I have a presence in the office in the middle of the week consistently.

My work hours also help provide the illusion on being in the office full-time. My work hours are from six am to three thirty pm. I normally get in the office around four which is still early in the day especially in the summer months because of the extended day light to service clients. If you have ever paid attention to the market the home sales are more aggressive in the summer months than in the winter. My clients are at work when I am at work so with that being said in order for them to buy a home they are working as well. Clients tend to call me for appointments on the afternoon hours and on weekends. Weekend appointments are the best for me and I try to service at least 5 or more clients in one day. Yes, you can serve as many as five clients if you master time management.

The car you drive could also provide you with time saving measures because it can become your office on wheels. I drive my van to work and it became my office on wheels equipped with lock boxes forms, signs and power tools. You see, no matter what happens I have what I need to maximize the time that I was afforded. I can receive a call to show a home after work and it just so happen to be near the neighborhood of one of my listing which allows me the opportunity to check on my signs and other things pertaining to my listing and if the sign needs some repair I can just take care of it right away because remember I keep my tools in the van that I drive. While at work my van allows me the privacy to make calls on my lunch and speak freely while eating my lunch at the same time, remember dual purpose activities.

My advice to agents that want to produce or create the volume of a complete full-time agent you must master time management and know that every minute counts. Time blocking works early in the morning I find but after about 10am each day my phone starts to ring and then I just roll with it. I grew up in my household with the phrase "the early bird gets the worm". If you wait later in the day to do something it will take you longer because now you are among all other late comers and now you must wait your turn.

Know When to Grow

As a dual career agent you have to know when to grow your business. I grew my business for over 20 years as a dual career agent before I took on a full-time hire. I paced myself and mastered time management skills to survive and support my business as it grew. Staying focused on what I wanted to accomplish and looking back on all things that did not work for me as a lesson learn event. I would always look at myself as self-motivated with a mental vision board embedded in my head.

I would also set goals for myself and the goals had to make sense and must be attainable. If you set goals too high and you don't reach them then you may become frustrated and then give up before reaching your goals. I would always say to myself I will put twenty percent effort and expect eighty percent return. It was somewhat tough to manage all as the business grew but I pushed through it because the growth in the beginning was not consistent. I would often say to myself that I can do it and then I did. Waking up each morning early will allow me before work to picture my day and remind myself to just roll with the punches.

My family would be my support when I needed it. It was hard in the beginning leaving my son at home with his father as I grew the real estate business until one day I decided to bring him along. My son was an assistant to my business because it taught him strong work ethics and the importance of sacrifice and discipline. I was always telling him you are in training for the business Olympics. Think of yourself as an Olympian that will practice over 16 hours a day and will eat sleep and drink their craft to master it and that's what I did to have the volume of a full-time agent and continue to grow and I am still growing. My extended family members also chipped in to help along with my husband and it became a family affair. At the end of the year I would reward everyone with a trip on me which allow us to grow and have fun as a family (again dual purposed activity). My son is now an agent and my husband, son and I have all fallen in love with real estate and will buy and fix homes together.

Staying as healthy as a possibly now has its requirements because my business is still growing so I had to take another look at how I should grow. I hired based on a business model that my broker introduced to me and hired 2 administrative positions. I wanted to hire for some time but I pushed it back until I knew that I could keep the staff on for as long as the business exists. I never wanted to hire someone and then they based their livelihood on me being able to pay them and then have to let them go because of my lack of planning. With me all things are math because numbers don't lie.

I am now looking into and forming a team model with the majority to all of team members that are dual career agents. The ability to share how I got to this point in volume and wanting to stay on my job because I love what I do, the team of dual career agents will afford me the opportunity to still grow and work on my full-time job as long I need to or want to. Retirement is in sight but I have not made the decision on date and time yet. Your decision to love both a full-time job and any business is totally up to you but just know it has its challenges and requires more. To build a business before you retire will allow you to have an easy transition with little to know financial gaps. There will be no start up loans to get started because you build as you go.

Your increase is in your Passion

I don't know how many times I have heard advise about how a person can increase the profits in their business. All the advice I've heard always leads back to passion. Let's look at the word passion, and what it means.

Passion: *an extremely strong feeling; often resulting in obsessive behavior.* Passion will have you thinking about what you love to do and it will not appear to be as work, but it will take on a feeling of being satisfied.

I wake up each morning, after my meditation time of gratefulness and focusing of my family. Then, my mind will focus on my real estate business. Having a clear mind in the morning allows me to have clarity and calmness with my daily direction.

Passion will bring you rewards. In other words, what you focus on will grow, weather it positive or negative. Believing in yourself and smiling through each task will grow into increase. Why talk about the word increase? Because, for me, I know if I work in my passion, the increase will come. That's just how passion works. In my 20 or more years in real-estate, I have watched so many new agents leave after a year, because their business in not growing, and the cost of doing business, along with frustration, has over taken the feeling of passion. I do believe you can create passion to a degree, but I also believe that passion is a part placed in you and why you were put on earth. I love to see flowers, but I don't have a green thumb. However, if I read and study about flowers, I will learn where to position it in the sun and how much water and fertilizer it needs to cause it to grow. I use this same technique into increasing my real estate business. In my business I have taking classes, read books, attend seminars, circle myself around other agents in the industry and try to learn something everyday no matter how small. The increase will show in your business if you constantly take care of your flower (your business). The consistency can help grow the passion because it will allow practices, procedures and result to begin to show up naturally.

Daily routine can become a habit and a habit will allow you to master the skill set for increase. A daily retune can build up a skill set that will take your business to another level and then your business will make room for you. A routine will bring a consistency that will eventually become natural. In my business, I have noticed that the passion I have for real estate is about the same feeling of passion that I have for supporting customers on my nine to five job. I truly believe you can have more than one passion and be successful in both. I wake up each morning knowing that I have more than one passion and I work in all of them and all of them bring me Increase. I created my own recipe for a passion driven set.

Increase Passion Pie: Recipe

1 Cup of gratefulness
½ Cup of patience with yourself
½ Cup of persistence
1Tbsp consistency
1Tbsp vision
½ tsp believe
½ tsp focus
½ tsp of faith
And a little bit of your secret ingredient of this and that

Mix the major ingredients of gratefulness, patience with yourself and persistence together each morning cover and let it rise for a few hours. After a few hours you will feel a self-fulfillment growing in side of you. Set aside your major ingredients and them mix in a separate bowl consistency, vision, believe, focus and faith. After your major ingredients have risen create a whole in the risen product to pure into the other ingredients and then fold over to knead together. When all ingredients are combined tougher you should not be able to see one ingredient separate from the other. When all things work together the end result will be satisfying to the taste. So when you crave for a different taste then just add that last ingredient of a little be more of this and that.

The Pie can represent many streams of passion. Picture of a pie

One sliced: Real Estate
Two Slices: Nine to Five
Third Slice: Flipping Homes
Fourth Slice: Being an Investor
Filth Slice: Being able to provide for Family
Sixth Slice: This and That

Spirituality

In a prior chapter, I talked about passion and increase. Now, I will share with you how I add spirituality to create a recipe for my success. In life, you will have to make many choices. And, if your choices are tied to your spiritual beliefs and destiny, they will return good for you. This was difficult for me to write, because it was hard for me to explain how I am so blessed with a growing business. I often feel as if I don't deserve my success.

I know after reading that last sentence you are probably saying to yourself why would she feel that way. Don't we all deserve the favor of the God we serve? I often question my thinking about this. I often ask myself why me. Why have I been able to work both a full-time job and also run a very successful real estate business with just hard work and passion? One day the answer to my question came clear to me. Whether you are as Christian, as I am, or not, every religion has the same "golden rule". For Christians, it's "give and it will be given back to you." For Hindus, it's Karma. The spiritual principle is the same; your present treatment of people determines the future treatment you will receive.

Being a servant to God to other with your talents and passion will return good to you. I was taught by my parents and within the church that I should share what I have been blessed with. I truly believe we all have something we can share that can help someone else. I know we have all heard a closed hand cannot receive but an open hand that gives also has room in the hand to receive.

I have mentioned several times about being grateful and meditation as part of my daily ritual. When I spend time in mediation, I can often get clarity about the direction I need to take in my business. I have attended many seminars and lectures, and more often than not, I will leave there saying to myself that I am on the right tract. The speaker will always touch on inner-peace, beliefs and faith. When you are connected with your spirituality side, I will wager that it will be of good nature and good success which come from it. I know that if I have more than enough, then I am truly blessed, and I should share.

I am currently at a real estate brokerage that believes in the golden rule of blessings and sharing which helps with productivity. When we have new agents come on board, a info session is held so they can hear from the other agents of how we all share and care about each other businesses. I never thought I would witness that in the business world, but I see it on a day to day basis in my brokerage.

When I put all my beliefs and faith in knowing that I am not doing this without help from a spiritual standpoint it always shows up with an increase for my business. I have a sense of gratefulness in all things big or small. All action and blessing in my business are seen as stepping stones to a greater good for myself and my business.

To trust myself spiritually and spend time growing in my beliefs allows me to walk in favor of God. When asked how I grow my business with less time than recommended for lead generation, my answer is puzzling to others at first. I tell them, I release the energy of gratefulness, truthfulness, happiness and faithfulness. Early on, in my real estate career, I read an article of how to become a money magnet. The principles in that article stuck with me. They were "reaping" and "sowing". The reward is in the belief and acting on the belief. Having a direct connection with my spirituality has allowed me the ability to lead generate every waken moment. Sometimes, I can't explain how the having favor over my life and my business will always show up just when I need it to.

Customer Service

Customer Service plays a very important part of my business. I always try to treat my clients the way I want to be treated. Making someone feels as if they are the most important person to me has been my way of providing the best customer service I can provide. It has always been a pet peeve of mind to interact with a person not providing top customer service. I know for me, I will not give them repeat business. I expect no less than great customer service, for my hard earned money.

I use customer service as my main lead generating tool. I have noticed that when you provide good customer service it will take you far. As a dual career agent, I don't have the ability to lead generate with cold call in the mornings, because I am at work. Also, the weekend is used for servicing my clients. Lead generating has just taken a different activity for me. When you perform an exceptional job the news can travel just like a cold call, promotional card mailer or any other lead generating product.

I try to answer every phone call and address each email on a timely manner. Most customers call on their lunch time, evenings after they get home from work or after they take care of the evening family chores. I will answer my cell up to 11pm at night accepting text or phone call from any client. I will ask the question of their preferred form of communication whether it phone calls, texting or email, and make a note of it.

It is important for me to meet with each client face to face. In a face to face meeting, it allows both parties the opportunity to make eye contact and get a better sense of the other person's temperament. The is very difficult to do with other forms of communication. I believe that the face to face meeting will allow me the opportunity to extract information about the nature of the business which is very important in having a smooth transactional relationship. I can't tell you how many times that I have obtained some information from the buyer or seller client that would have caused us some problems down the road because they did not know that the information was important to the transaction.

When meeting with my clients, I will always tell them my working hours, which are seven days a week and Sunday after church. My seven days a week sounds like I never have time for myself, but that couldn't be further from the truth. Remember in the earlier chapters, I talked about having most of all your actions as dual purpose actions. I just believe you can have both. Hopefully, you've learned to turn your *"this or that"* statements into *"this and that"*.

I have monitored and tract my lead sources and over eighty percent (80%) of my leads to new clients are generated because of my customer service to previous clients. I have many past clients letting me know that they will shout my name from the mountain tops because of the service I provided them. I heavily rely on their good words about my service, and I let them know how much I would appreciate them recommending me to their coworker, fiend and family. I don't use the electronic or print marketing tools. I want to make sure my nine to five employer doesn't have the perception that every time I take off from work they will think that I am doing real-estate or that I don't need a promotion because I have a side business. Remember, I am trying to keep my employment separate from my business, and for over twenty years or more that has worked for me. I am not saying the marketing material are not important, I just have to be careful with how I market. As I mentioned earlier, your best lead generator is by providing great customer service.

A Typical Day

As I come to a close in my writings I would like to share with you what a typical day looks like for me as I implement my techniques, policies and procedures.

I start each day with a form of meditation and gratefulness and thanksgiving to my beliefs. This could take me a few minutes to more than a half an hour it depends on if I overslept for work or not. Let's remember I am a secret agent. While in meditation, I plan my day with what I would like to accomplish but let's be clear it never goes as planned so I just adjust and go with it. However, planning my day in my head still allows me to accomplish a lot more than just going through the day with no direction.

I then prepare for work and totally dedicate the rest of my morning to getting to work on time. While driving to work I get back into my secret place of gratefulness and thanksgiving. I start focusing in on what I need to accomplish during my lunch time at work. My lunch time is often full with returning phone calls and emails from my own laptop. I take my mobile hot spot and find a quiet place to work most times in my van without distractions because I only have thirty minutes for lunch. I have turned my form of transportation into a mobile office.

When my 9 to 5 work day ends, I prepare my plans for what I need to accomplish when I get to my real estate office. If I can I will show properties when I leave my 9 to 5 job all the way to my office so I can maximize my time traveled and the ability to service a client or meet a potential customer. The ability to map my way to the office allows me to save on time, gas and wear and tear on my car. If you remember in my writings I mentioned that I try to make each technique, policy and procedure dual purpose.

I normally get into my real estate office around early afternoon if there are no showings on the way. After arriving in the office, I would have already jotted down my to-do list as tasks come to me throughout the day. I keep a spiral tablet with me always which allows me to see how much I accomplished in a day and who and what services I provided. I began to work off my to-do list that I developed and remain open minded to all adjustments that will happen daily.

I normally leave the office around nine pm and within that time I would have try to accomplish as much on my list as I could and sometimes taking time to exercises by just walking around my office building to clear my head as well as get in a form of exercise. Leaving the office only to get home and put myself in a meditation state of gratefulness to be able to accomplish what I could and to have the opportunity to try again tomorrow.

I conclude this guide with the message of asking yourself are you willing to put in the work and implement some of the items that I discussed here. I have more to tell and would love to coach you or speak to you in a workshop setting so we can grow your business whether its real estate or any other business. There are large amounts of brokerages that have secret and dual career agents and this guide I hope can help grow your business which in turn helps grow the market centers and brokerages which creates a win-win.

About The Author

Wanda Russell is the CEO of *WD Russell Real Estate Inc.*® and President of *The Russell Group*. She has been in the real estate business for over 20 years. She is licensed in Maryland, District of Columbia, Virginia and Delaware for residential and commercial properties.

Wanda is a member of:

- The National Association of Realtors
- Keller Williams Realty International (KWRI)
- Maryland Association of Realtors
- Prince Georges County (MD) Association of Realtor
- Sussex County (Delaware) Association of Realtors
- Women's Council of Realtors
- Real Estate Ladies Rock

For teaching seminars, speaking engagements and coaching please contact her at:

Wanda Russell
P.O. Box 4462,
Kettering, MD 20775
Direct: 301.704.5259
WDRussellRE@gmail.com

Made in the USA
Columbia, SC
08 February 2018